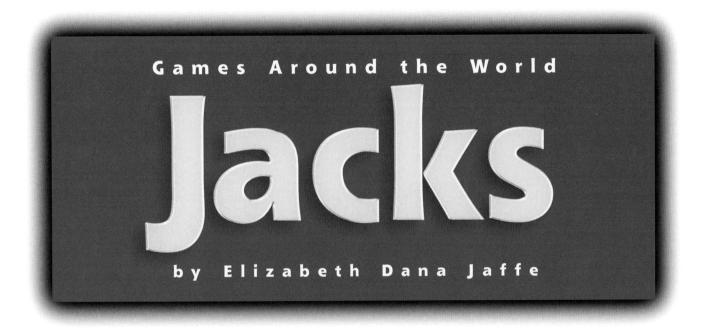

Games Around the World

Jacks

by Elizabeth Dana Jaffe

Content Adviser: Professor Sherry L. Field, Department of Social Science Education, College of Education, The University of Georgia

Reading Adviser: Dr. Linda D. Labbo, Department of Reading Education, College of Education, The University of Georgia

COMPASS POINT BOOKS

MINNEAPOLIS, MINNESOTA

Compass Point Books
3722 West 50th Street, #115
Minneapolis, MN 55410

Visit Compass Point Books on the Internet at *www.compasspointbooks.com* or e-mail your request to
custserv@compasspointbooks.com

Photographs ©: Gregg Andersen, cover, 5, 10, 13, 26; TRIP/J.
Highet, 4; Erich Lessing/Art Resource, NY, 6; Archivo
Iconografico, S.A./Corbis, 7; Hulton Getty/Archive
Photos, 8; International Stock/Steve Meyers, 9.

Editors: E. Russell Primm and Emily J. Dolbear
Photo Researcher: Svetlana Zhurkina
Photo Selector: Linda S. Koutris
Designer: Bradfordesign, Inc.
Illustrator: Abby Bradford

Library of Congress Cataloging-in-Publication Data

Jaffe, Elizabeth D.
    Jacks / by Elizabeth Dana Jaffe content adviser, Sherry L. Field ; reading adviser, Linda D. Labbo.
        p. cm. — (Games around the world)
    Includes bibliographical references and index.
    ISBN 0-7565-0134-2 (hardcover : lib. bdg.)
        1. Jacks (Game)—Juvenile literature. [1. Jacks (Game) 2. Games.] I. Field, Sherry L. II. Labbo, Linda D.
III. Title.
    GV1215.7 .J34 2002
    796.2—dc21   2001001593

Table of Contents

Playing Jacks

"**Onesies, twosies, threesies**, . . ." You must be playing **jacks**! You can play jacks alone or with friends. You can play jacks indoors or outside. All you need is a ball, some jacks, and a smooth, flat surface to play on.

A jack is a playing piece with six points, or legs. Each jack rests on three legs so it is easy to pick up. Beginners should start with five jacks. With practice, you can work your way up to ten!

Once you know the basics, you can make up your own rules and games. Remember, playing jacks is about having fun.

▲ *A ball and a jack*

◀ *Children in Kingston, Jamaica, play jacks in the street.*

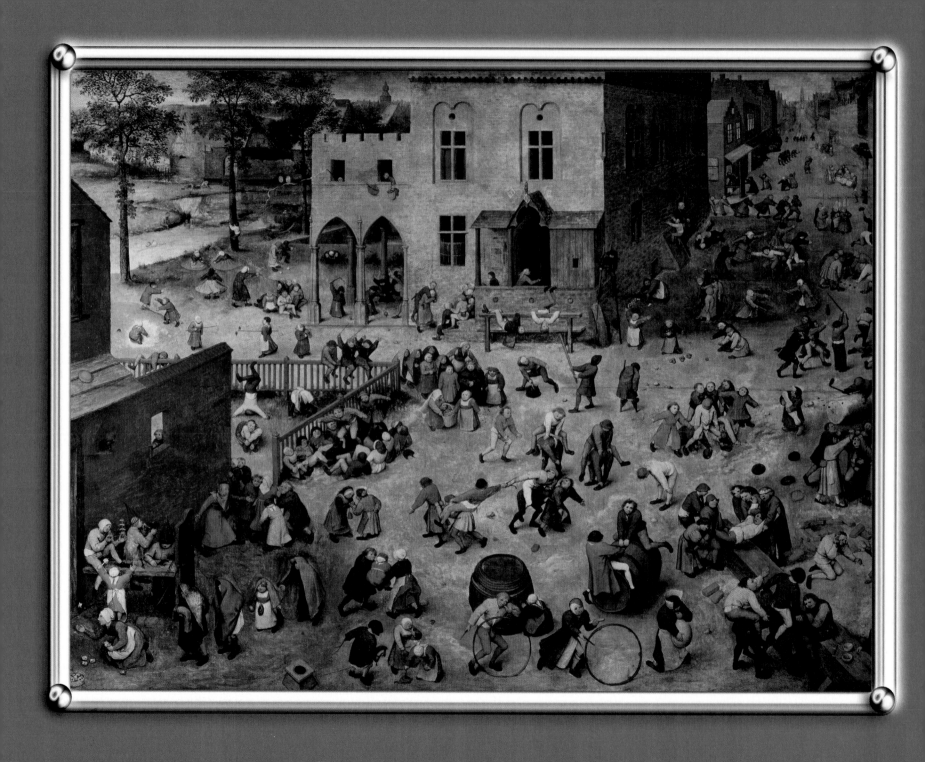

The History of Jacks

No one knows for sure *when* people first played jacks. No one knows *where* people first played jacks either. We do know that people around the world have played jacks for a long time.

About 2,500 years ago, people in Greece played a jacks game. They made the playing pieces out of sheep bones. These bones were called knucklebones. People also used them as dice. People played jacks in China and Russia too.

◀ Pieter Brueghel painted young people playing jackstones and other games in 1560.

▲ In this ancient Roman painting, women play knucklebones.

▲ *Two children play jacks outside a barbershop in Liverpool, England, in 1890.*

Long ago, the Romans used marble, glass, and valuable stones to play jacks. Roman soldiers brought the game with them to many countries, including England. There, children played jacks in the street.

The English brought jacks to America. In the 1800s, pioneer families played jacks as they traveled west. Today, American children still play jacks at home and on playgrounds.

People have made jacks from many different things. The first jacks were usually made from animal bones, shells, and stones. Wealthy people used valuable stones and ivory. Today, most jacks are made by machines. They are usually made of metal or plastic.

▲ Plastic jacks and a rubber ball

What Are Jacks Called?

The game of jacks has had many different names. People have called it jackstones, chackstones, dibs, knucklebones, or five stones.

How to Play Jacks

In most jacks games, you toss an object into the air. Then you pick up the jacks from the ground while you catch the object in the air. You can use only one hand.

The tossed object is called a **jackstone**. In some games, the jackstone is a rubber ball. In other games, a jackstone is one of the playing pieces. If the jackstone is a ball, the player can let it bounce only once. If the jackstone is a playing piece, the player must catch it before it hits the ground.

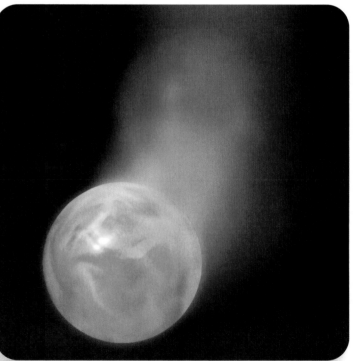

▲ Remember, the ball can only bounce once!

Jacks are played in **rounds**.
A round is a cycle of play in which
each player gets a turn. To start
most rounds, a player **scatters**, or
throws, the jacks across the ground.

In jacks, the rounds are called
onesies, twosies, threesies, and so on up

▲ *Scattered jacks and a ball*

to the highest round—tensies. That's a
game with ten jacks. The player has to
pick up all ten jacks. In onesies, the
player picks up one jack at a time.
Then he or she moves on to the next
round. The next round is twosies. In
twosies, the player picks up two jacks
at a time.

▲ *In onesies, you pick up one jack at a time.*

11

Jacks Do's and Don'ts

- Pick one spot and play the whole game from that spot. Choose a comfortable position to play from.

- Scatter all jacks with one hand in a smooth motion. Scatter them so that they are spaced for easy pickup. Remember you want more space between the jacks for onesies than for tensies.

- Control the height and direction of your toss of the jackstone. You need time to pick up the jacks and catch the jackstone easily.

- Don't let the ball or jacks touch your clothing or body except for your playing hand. (That's called clothes burn.)

- Don't touch any jacks you aren't trying to pick up. (That's called touchies.)

- Don't separate jacks that are on top of each other. (They are called haystacks.)

- Don't separate jacks that are touching. (They are called kissies.)

- Don't drop the ball or jacks that you have already picked up. (That's called drops.)

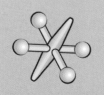

In threesies, the player picks up three jacks at a time. There will be one jack left. That jack is called the **cart**. The player picks up the left-over jack or jacks last. The player continues all the way to tensies.

If you make a mistake, your turn is over. You start your next turn on the round where you left off.

▲ *Be careful not to make any mistakes.*

Playing for Funsies and Strictsies

You can play jacks for **funsies** or **strictsies**. Funsies'
rules make the game easier. Playing for funsies
is a good way to learn to play jacks.

Playing for funsies means you can **dub**.

That means you can
move the
jacks before
you pick
them up.

▲ *Sometimes jacks scatter
too far apart.*

You can also
call "**overs**." That means if you don't
like your first throw, you can scatter the
jacks again.

▲ *In funsies, you can move the
jacks closer together.*

Strictsies' rules make the game harder. In strictsies, you must scatter your jacks at least a hand's width apart.

In strictsies, no matter how the jacks scattered, you have to **one grab**. That means you have to pick up all the jacks in one smooth sweep of your hand.

▲ *A hand's width*

▲ *One grab*

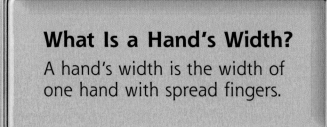

What Is a Hand's Width?
A hand's width is the width of one hand with spread fingers.

15

Flipping—Who Goes First?

Before you start a game of jacks, you have to decide who goes first. One way to decide is to **flip** jacks.

There are several ways to flip. To flip with both hands, cup your hands together with the pinkies touching. Put the jacks in your hands.

▲ *Hold the jacks in your hands.*

Toss the jacks straight up. Flip your hands over quickly. Put your hands together with forefingers touching. (Your forefinger is next to your thumb.) Catch the jacks on the backs of your hands.

Then toss the jacks into the air again. Flip your hands back over. Catch the jacks in your cupped hands. You can flip with one hand too.

▲ *Then catch the jacks on the back of your hands.*

16

When you flip jacks, you are trying to catch as many jacks as you can. The player who catches the most jacks goes first. In a tie, players flip until one player catches more jacks than the other.

▲ *Then catch the jacks in your hands again.*

Flipping Do's and Don'ts

- Try to keep all jacks bunched up together.

- When catching on the backs of both hands, put your hands in a V.

- When catching on the back of one hand, spread your fingers out.

- Don't toss the jacks too high.

Jumpin' Jacks—A Game from America

This is the basic jacks game. Children play this game in the United States and Canada.

Number of players: One or more

What you need: Ten jacks and a small rubber ball

Object: To go from onesies to tensies and back down again

How to play:

1. Scatter ten jacks on the ground.

2. The first round is onesies. The first player must pick up all ten jacks, one at a time. You can't miss or drop a jack. You must catch the ball after one bounce. Put each jack you pick up into the other hand, or set it aside.

3. After you have picked up all ten jacks, scatter all the jacks again. Begin the next round—twosies.

4. If you don't make any mistakes, go on to the next round.

5. If you make a mistake, you are out. Then it is the next player's turn.

6. The first player to play up to tensies and back down to onesies wins!

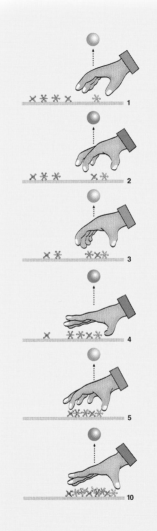

Kong-Keui—A Game from South Korea

This game has three rounds. It is played in Asia. Boys usually play with stones or brick pieces. Girls usually play with coins. You can use jacks instead.

Number of players: Two or more

What you need: Five jacks

Object: To finish the three rounds first

How to play:

ROUND 1 is called *al-nat-ki*, or "laying the eggs."

1. Scatter four jacks on the ground.

2. Throw the fifth jack (the jackstone) in the air.

3. Pick up one jack. Then catch the jackstone before it hits the ground.

4. Put the jack you just picked up aside.

5. Repeat steps 2 and 3 until you have picked up all four jacks and put them aside. You have now "laid your eggs."

▲ *Throw the fifth jack in the air.*

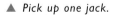

▲ *Pick up one jack.*

▲ *And catch the jackstone!*

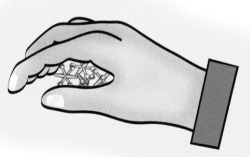

▲ Toss the jackstone in the air and push one jack under your cupped hand.

ROUND 2 is called *al-hpoum-ki*, or "setting the eggs."

6. Cup your hand on the ground next to the four jacks.

7. Toss the jackstone with your other hand.

8. Push one jack under your cupped hand. Then catch the jackstone.

9. Continue until all four jacks are under your cupped hand. Your "eggs" have now been "set."

▲ Your eggs are "set."

ROUND 3 is called *al-kka-ki*, or "hatching the eggs."

10. Put three jacks on the ground.

11. Put the fourth jack in the fold of your pinky on the outside of your throwing hand.

▲ *Toss the jackstone and tap a jack with the jack in your pinky.*

12. Toss the fifth jack (the jackstone).

13. Tap a jack on the ground with the jack in your pinky. Then catch the jackstone.

14. Continue until you have tapped all three jacks. Your "eggs" have now been "hatched."

15. The first player to finish all three rounds is the winner.

▲ *Then catch the jack while holding the jack in your pinky.*

Osselets—A Game from Haiti

Haiti is an island in the Caribbean. Children in Haiti play this game with **osselets**. Osselets are playing pieces made from animal knuckles. You can use jacks instead. Some children use a jack instead of a ball. Then you have to catch the jack before it hits the ground.

Number of players:	One or more
What you need:	Five jacks and a small rubber ball
Object:	To finish the three rounds first
How to play:	
1.	Put the ball and five jacks in your throwing hand.
2.	Throw the ball and jacks into the air. Let the jacks fall to the ground. Catch the ball after one bounce.

3. Throw the ball. Pick up one jack. Catch the ball. Keep this jack in the throwing hand.

4. Throw the ball. Pick up a second jack. Catch the ball. Keep this jack in the throwing hand too.

5. Continue until you have picked up all five jacks in your throwing hand.

6. The first player to do this wins.

▲ *Throw five jacks and the ball in the air.*

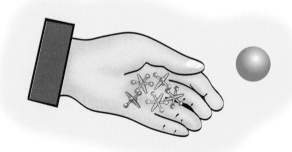

▲ *All jacks in throwing hand*

What Is Your Fancy?

When you get good at jacks, try adding a **fancy**. A fancy is an extra round at the end of a game. It makes the game a little harder. Jack Be Nimble, Around the World, or Black Widow are some fancies.

You can also make up your own fancies. The rules of jacks may change over time, but the game will always be about having fun.

▲ *Make up your own rules!*

Some Fancies

Around the World
Toss the ball. Pick up the jacks. Circle the bouncing ball with your throwing hand. Catch the ball before it bounces.

Black Widow
Play onesies to tensies without missing. If you miss, you have to start over at onesies again. Try going from onesies to tensies and back again.

Jack Be Nimble
Toss the ball up and say "Jack be nimble." Touch the ground and catch the ball. Do it again but say "Jack be quick." Then toss the ball up and say "Jack jumped over." Touch the ground on both sides of a jack and catch the ball. Then throw the ball up and say "the candlestick." Pick up the jack and catch the ball.

Glossary

cart—the leftover jack or jacks in a round of jacks

dub—to move the jacks before picking them up

fancy—an extra round added to a jacks game to make it harder

flip—to throw jacks in the air and catch them on your hands

funsies—a way to play jacks where the rules make the game easier

jacks—plastic or metal playing pieces with six points

jackstone—the ball or jack a player tosses in the air while picking up the jacks from the ground

onesies—the first round of jacks when a player picks up the jacks one at a time

one grab—to pick up all the jacks in one smooth sweep of the hand

osselets—playing pieces made from animal knuckles

overs—if a player doesn't like his or her throw, the player calls "overs" and scatters jacks again

rounds—cycles of play

scatter—to throw jacks on the ground with one hand in a smooth motion

strictsies—a way to play jacks where the rules make the game harder

threesies—the third round of jacks when the player picks up the jacks three at a time

twosies—the second round of jacks when the player picks up the jacks two at a time

Did You Know?

* The word *jacks* comes from England.

* In the ancient Roman city called Pompeii, a drawing on a building shows women playing jacks.

* If something unfair happens during a jacks game, you can call "interference" and go again.

Want to Know More?

At the Library

Chabert, Sally. *The Jacks Book*. New York: Workman Publishing, 1999.

Erlbach, Arlene. *Sidewalk Games Around the World*. Brookfield, Conn.: Millbrook Press, 1997.

Gryski, Camilla. *Let's Play: Traditional Games of Childhood*. Buffalo, N.Y.: Kids Can Press, 1998.

Lankford, Mary D. *Jacks: Around the World*. New York: Morrow Junior Books, 1996.

Martin, Ann M. *Little Sister: Playground Games*. New York: Scholastic, Inc. 1996.

On the Web

Jacks

http://www.gameskidsplay.net/games/jacks_and_marbles_etc/jacks.htm

For the basic rules of jacks

Parentcenter.com: Jacks

http://www.parentcenter.com/refcap/fun/games/7410/7498/14130.html

For the basic rules of jacks and links to other games

Streetplay.com: The Games, Jacks

http://www.streetplay.com/thegames/jacks/

For the basic rules of jacks and an illustration of the jacks pickup technique

Through the Mail

Toy Manufacturers of America, Inc.

1115 Broadway

Suite 400

New York, NY 10010

To order a copy of a booklet on toy safety called *Fun Play, Safe Play*

On the Road

Canadian Children's Museum

at the Canadian Museum of Civilization

100 Laurier Street

Hull, Quebec J8X 4H2

Canada

819/776-8294

To visit an exhibit with old and new toys and games from around the world

Index

About the Author

After graduating from Brown University, Elizabeth Dana Jaffe received her master's degree in early education from Bank Street College of Education. Since then, she has written and edited educational materials. Elizabeth Dana Jaffe lives in New York City.